Hitting Bone

Also by Jackie L. Disch

Life Forces a Journey

Hitting Bone

※

Jackie L. Disch

JLD Publishing
Minneapolis, Minnesota

Copyright © 2004 by Jackie L. Disch

All rights reserved. No part of this book may be reproduced or transmitted in any form or by any means, electronic or mechanical, including photocopy, recording, or any information storage and retrieval system, without permission in writing from the publisher – except in the case of brief quotations used in critical articles or reviews.

Requests for permission to make copies of any part of the work – except where permitted above – should be mailed to the following address: Permissions Department, JLD Publishing, P.O. Box 24231, Minneapolis, Minnesota 55424. You may also contact the publisher online at www.jldpublishing.com or by e-mail: info@jldpublishing.com.

Quote from *Bird by Bird,* © 1994 by Anne Lamott, reprinted with the permission of the Wylie Agency, Inc.

ISBN: 0-9710842-1-1

Library of Congress Control Number: 2004092357

First Printing

Printed in the United States of America by Morris Publishing
3212 East Highway 30 • Kearney, NE 68847
1-800-650-7888

To Tami and Donna –
For your remarkable support and friendship

To Cheryl –
An unsuspecting contributor to the
creation of this book

And to Everyone at LHC – especially
Linda, Kostas, Darby, Shannon and Heather –
For moving me to beauty

Contents

I
If You Play With a Loaded Gun
You're Bound to Get Shot

Trilingual	1
Emotional Demons	2
If You Play With a Loaded Gun You're Bound to Get Shot	3
Hollow Daze	4
Mourning Routine	5
Silent Pain Deep Down	6
Better and Worse	7
Prisoner	8
There is a Hole	9
She Has Spent Her Life Dying	10
Wedged in a Knot	12
Growing Up	13
Ultimate Silence	14
Shutting You Out	15
Fine Line	16
Changing Time	18
Tormented	19
Dilemma	20
I Lost My Place	21

Coward in the Face of Kindness	22
Flailing	23

II
Hitting Bone

Nightmare	27
Spell Bound	28
Timelessness	29
The Road to Freedom	30
Voices From Within	31
Bought and Sold	32
Before She Moves On	33
This Time of Year, Past	34
The Rationale and Reality of Violence	35
The Abuser's Holy Trinity	36
Once Upon a Child	37
Hitting Bone	38
The Beating Mantra	39
Through the Gates	40
Disappearing	42
In a World	43
Graceless	44
Domestic Disturbance	45

Time-Ax	46
Blackout II	47
Oblivion	48
Dreamless	49

III
At Times I'm Moved to Beauty

Believing	53
Searching for the Light	54
Maybe	55
Learning to Live	56
Mid-Summer Musing	57
The Cold Wind	58
Hospital Visit	59
Subsequent Visits: The Kissing Lips	61
Rummaging Around	62
In Limbo	63
What Truth Does She Hold	65
Tagged	66
Poem on the Run	67
No More Freud	68
Shoes	69
Crumbling	70

To Be Free Is All I Ever Really Wanted	71
The Lost and Found	72
Molten Rocket	73
Blood, Snakes, and Mayonnaise	74
At Times I'm Moved to Beauty: A poem inspired by Emily Dickinson, Edna St. Vincent Millay, and Sylvia Plath	75
Diamond in the Rough	76

To the Reader

Hitting Bone was born in my therapist's office about a year and a half ago while exploring myself and the world around me. Some of the poems included in this collection were written several years ago and some are recent. All of them contribute to the process of "hitting bone."

Jackie L. Disch
May 2004

Good writing is about telling the truth. We are a species that needs and wants to understand who we are.
                                        - Anne Lamott

Hitting Bone

I

If You Play With a Loaded Gun You're Bound to Get Shot

Trilingual

Verbally
I say little
or nothing at all

but my eyes
and my body
have languages
all their own

and every-once-in-a-while
through them -
the story of my life
is told.

Emotional Demons

I battle emotional demons
that threaten to tear me apart.

They come alive in my head,
make me wish I were dead,
and ravage what's left of my heart.

They are the ghosts of my past
haunting me still
reminders of lessons well learned.

And when they are near
I am consumed in fear
of memories that still burn.

If You Play With a Loaded Gun
You're Bound to Get Shot

I'm only doing this for
your own good.
Click
BANG

How did you get to
be so stupid.
Click
BANG

How many times have
I told you!
Click
BANG

If you weren't so clumsy.
Click
BANG

I don't want to have
to tell you again.
Click
BANG

Come here and help
me with this.
Click
BANG

Don't you ever listen?
Click
BANG

You make me sick.
Click
BANG

I'll give you something
to cry about.
Click
BANG

Get away from me.
Click
BANG

If you had a brain
you'd be dangerous.
Click
BANG

Where did you learn to
talk like that?
Click
BANG

Why are you always
doing this to me?
Click
BANG

You have to grow up
sometime. I'm not always
going to be around to take
care of you.

Hollow Daze

He passes most days in silence
thinking thoughts he can't see
clearly sometimes
through the drug induced haze
he sometimes still feels
the claws tearing his skin
but no he never really felt it
not the searing pain
that should have been there
more like a dull tug
dull very dull
like an after thought
of things to come
He thought he heard himself
scream as he thought he felt
the claws tearing open
his skin but no it must
have been someone else
some place else screaming
there are eighteen years of
drugs running through his veins
hypnotic he fades in and out
and then he's gone thinking
he feels pain thinking he hears
screams yeah he hears you
yeah he knows what you are talking
about but you see he can't
keep his eyes open they
shot him too full this time
I can't help you, he says
I'm sorry
I can't help

Mourning Routine

I wake up every morning
in terror and dread
of what the day will bring.

How much emotional pain
will rip through me?
How much torment
will I be in?

Will I reach my breaking point today?

How bad will things be today?
At what else will I fail today?

How much anger and hatred
will eat away at my heart?
How much will I lose today?

Will today be the day
where I'll have had enough?
And if so,
what will tomorrow be like?

And then I get up.

Silent Pain Deep Down

Silent
Pain
Deep
Down
Hold
Tight
Wave
After
Wave
Panics
Soul
Not
Safe
Must
Hide
Silent
Pain
Deep
Down.

Better and Worse

I was told
it would probably get worse
before it got better.

I didn't believe –
thought I had the control.

It's been frightening
to find I don't.

My mind – my body
have built ways
to protect and serve themselves.

Now, I am a bystander,
though I am certainly
not innocent.

Now, I wait
for things to get
better.

Prisoner

I am a prisoner
in a cage
trying sometimes
to free myself
only to find
the cage is self-made
and I've lost the key.

There is a Hole

In my heart
there is a hole
    so deep
that it touches
the core
    of eternity
And it is empty
except for
    the ache
of loneliness
    which tears me
        apart.

She Has Spent Her Life Dying

She has spent her life dying.

She has finally realized
since her birth in this life
each second passed
has been spent dying.

All of her time and energy
"growing up"
was spent numbing herself -
deadening all her feelings
emotions, desires, dreams,
thoughts, questions -
holding onto herself
and only herself.

Building her own world
Building her own reality
Building her own casket

    wanting to die
    needing to die
    almost dying

It is all she has known.
The gift
given to her
at birth.

The lessons taught (learned)
    love (is pain)
    trust (is forbidden)
    respect (is impossible)
    mistakes (punishable by death)

The rules constantly changed.

Life, she learned,
was a game
she could not win
and did not deserve to play.

Wedged in a Knot

My whole body
        weeps
from all
it has known

And yet the
        tears
never reach
my eyes

Instead
they remain
firmly lodged
        in my throat

Wedged
in a knot of
        unrelenting
emotion

Growing Up

The aches and pains
of growing up
      getting older, staying tough
are sometimes hard
      and unbearable
but I always seem to find I'm able

To endure and ensure
my continuing days
      though I know it's not easy
      with my stubborn ways

Ultimate Silence

let the rage be —
suffocate it with
calmness
deny yourself
the experience
of letting it out
in a fury
of ultimate
silence.

Shutting You Out

I hear the closing of the door
that shuts you out —

   hard
         a little too hard
     harder than is meant.

I hear the resounding echo
I feel the reverberation move
through me like an aftershock.

It's safer this way,
              I tell myself —
It's better.

Behind this closed door,
I will not hear you
       when you walk away
I will not feel you leave

You will never leave, you say

You don't see that to me —
     you already have.

Fine Line

There is such a fine line
between apparent sanity
and insanity — one that
requires much coordination
and balance while walking it.

It would be very easy
to cross over the line
from acceptable behavior
to craziness.

Or would it simply be acting out?

Acting out of what?
        Self-hatred, Doubt,
        Ignorance, Stupidity,
        Fear, Desire?

The demands to know
what was wrong with me
went unfulfilled.
There were no answers —
only thousands of questions
that never got asked.

And now,
everything is alright — okay.
Guilt has made
acceptance possible —
denial still runs strong
bringing tolerance with it.

The truth
may never be known
to you
as it certainly is
not known to me.

I have questioned my sanity
for years now
because you
questioned my behavior.

There must be
something wrong with me
if there is nothing wrong
with you.

Except
things didn't really get better –
I simply covered them better
so that you – (and I) –
could not see.

And now,
everything is not alright – okay.
I don't know me anymore.
I don't know who I am.
My life has been a lie
and the truth
is difficult to find

while walking the fine line
you helped create.

Changing Time

The answer does not come
from the outside.

It comes from within.

Only then will time change
to an understandable concept

bringing together as one
the past
        the present
                and the future.

Tormented

I am tormented
in this life
by a past
that won't let me go
and a future
that denies forgiveness.

Forever trapped
in a process
in which I find
no relief —
only fear, pain, rage
when I dare
to open my eyes
and see.

Will things ever change?

Or am I destined
to a life
where I am tormented
trapped and haunted
by the memories
embedded in my soul.

Dilemma

She asks a question
and I hesitate.

There is no right or wrong
answer, she says.

She does not understand
my dilemma.

It is not that I'm afraid
of giving the wrong answer.

I'm afraid of answering
the wrong question.

I Lost My Place

I lost track of time
I lost my place
I lost my mark
    when I turned the page
when I turned my head
    when I turned to see
if you had turned your back on me
    in time to watch you disappear
    walking away, leaving me here
        leaving me trapped
            leaving me scared
leaving me almost convinced
                that you cared

Coward in the Face of Kindness

    don't show me compassion
        don't show me understanding
            don't show me gentleness
    don't be nice to me

I can't defend myself
    against attacks of kindness
    and if I have no defense
    then I will *feel*
        feelings I still can't cope with
        feelings I am still afraid of

if you show me compassion
    I will get angry with you
if you show me understanding
    I will hate you
if you show me gentleness
    I will fear you

    if you are nice to me
        you will destroy me

- in the face of kindness
        I am a coward –

Flailing

I heard a bird yell
"Scream!"
through the window.

I wish I could,
I answered silently.

"Listen to this"
said the bird —

and it let out a scream
heard, I'm sure,
for blocks around.

Then he sang
a little something
and moved on.

I wish I could
fly away.

II
Hitting Bone

Nightmare

There is no screaming
when the blade
enters deep.

There are no tears
to release
the unfelt pain.

The blood
is not recognized
as such.

All color has gone
out of life.

Spell Bound

bound to silence
        a vow of death
let not a whisper
        escape with my breath
let not a word
        pass through these lips
nor a sound be uttered
        I may regret

Instead
        let this ponderous pen
                that I hold
spell out in silence
        what cannot be told.

Timelessness

I am child, adolescent, adult
I am unborn yet alive in this world
I am female, male, neither, both
I have taken life to give life
Darkness is the light that guides me
My home is the Womb, the Tomb, this Room
I fear nothing and embrace the fear of others
I mark time by the Moon, the Stars, the Sun,
                              and the Seasons
In my world, Day follows Night follows Day
                              follows Night
The years mean little to me, vary little to me
Time is the Passage Way of Eternity
The Universe is my Playground but I do
not engage in childish games
For I have died a thousand Deaths
                              and still I live.

The Road to Freedom

The road to freedom
Is not paved with Glory;
It is paved with pain,
      Agony, anguish
And then flooded
      With an endless torrent
Of tears.

Voices From Within

Do not break the chain.
Do not break the cycle.

You cannot go
any further in your memory

we will stop you.

You hear us speak
listen
        to our words.

You will find no answers here
        only darkness
        silent blackness
        the scent of Death.

We live within you
have always been
we will remain (quiet)
if you leave well enough alone.

        Go no further –
        only emptiness waits
        on the other side.

You will have nothing
where once you had us.

Bought and Sold

You wear your pain well
though it's hidden in your eyes.
It isn't hard to tell
though it's covered by the lies.
It becomes you as a shadow
that vaguely leaves a trace
but you can tell there's been a battle
by the scars left on your face.
It all leaves you with the look
of a young one feeling old
by all the things they took
while you were bought and sold.

Before She Moves On

I can hear her screaming
through the passages of time.

It echoes in my mind.

Fear holds her motionless
while time continues on.

There is so much to forget
and even more to remember

before the time is gone,
before she can move on.

This Time of Year, Past

I stopped breathing
                    eyes shut

I stopped being
                    don't breath

until it was over
                    don't feel

until it was safe
                    don't move

until I knew
                    don't look

I could exhale life
                    back into myself.

The Rationale and Reality of Violence

The rationale:
    "It's okay, he's just blowing off steam."

The reality:
    it terrifies me

The rationale:
    "He was drunk."

The reality:
    he does it when he's not drunk

The rationale:
    "I'm sorry baby, I didn't mean to hurt you."

The reality:
    he always did.

The Abuser's Holy Trinity

Silence
is the golden rule
Ignorance
is bliss
Hope
will make you out
the fool
As something
you will miss.

Once Upon a Child

Once
>upon a Time
there was a
>>Child
>who lost her
>Mind
she lost her
>>Hope
>>she lost her
>>Will
>she lost her
>>Way
and in the still
>>of the night
when Darkness came
>>to claim her Life
>she lost her name

Hitting Bone

Like a needle
burrowing itself
into the infection
known as silence,
piercing the layers of lies
that covers with false comfort —

hitting bone

scraping away
at the matter
that matters most,
extracting the essence
of the misidentified pain
that is so easy to embrace
in place of truth.

An agonizing procedure —
but one that self-discovery
demands.

The Beating Mantra

I hold my heart in my hands
close to my chest

If I am going to be beaten
I'll be beaten by the best.

You can try to hold me,
you can try to pin me down

But before you can catch me,
you know I must be found.

Through the Gates

Through the Gates –
blood stains the steps down
Turning the dirty cement to
a rusty red-brown.
These stairs lead to a tunnel
an underground enclave
Where the Past dances in the dim light
and encapsulates us like a slave.
Guards stand by at the entrance
just below the stairs
Invisible to the naked eye
but the Guards are always there.
What happens in this dungeon –
in this room that never ends
Is a source of great discomfort
as the seasons pass again.

Lights flash like licks of fire
a stabbing pain of Truth
Lies buried in the slumber
trapped beneath this roof.
Dancing in the moonlight
that never reaches us
The darkness keeps us moving –
we'll either burst or bust.
Now visitors come a-knocking
what business do they hold?
By the time we are discovered
the Truth will be too old.
For suffering is an existence
that neither starts nor ends.
The cycle gets repeated
as the seasons pass again.

We cannot know the answers
as the questions are not asked
There is no rhyme or reason
when looking at the Past.
So, forgive me for not saying
what we all already know —
The Past it dances mercilessly
and Time, it passes slow.
Still we wonder what would happen
if we let somebody in
If we let the Guards stand down
and brightly lit what has been dim.
Would an avalanche up heave us?
Would our world come crashing in?
Would the cycle get repeated?
Would the seasons pass again?

There are bloodstains on our eyes
there is numbness in our hands
The Truth that we are bound to
no one would truly understand.
But the stakes are on the table
the chairs are chained in place
The door has been cracked open
and fear is on the plate.
Will the darkness be our savior?
Will the light be our demise?
Time is on the short end for
another season is on the rise.

Disappearing

endless
expansive
whiteness –

never-ending

isolation grips
emptiness seeps in
hunger gnaws
she becomes one
with the frigid blankness

it envelops her

trapped
in a tundra of fear –
broken and
brittle
she is forced into the whiteness
and disappears

In a World

In a world of silence
I have no name
In a world of violence
I feel no pain
In a world of illusion
I have no shame
In a world of accusation
I take all blame
In a world of betrayal
I get the same
In a world of portrayal
I play the game
In a world of condemnation
I do not complain.

Graceless

I did not fall from grace

  I   I

    was   was

      pushed

Domestic Disturbance

stripped
of the freedom
to be safe
in your own home,
in your own bed –

unable to trust,
to rest in peace
for even a moment.

is no place sacred?
in his eyes,
no –

married or not
he can rape you
just the same.

Time-Ax

Brother —
Can you spare the time?
I seem to have misplaced it
somewhere in my mind.
It was here just a moment ago
but the moment's passed
and well — you know —
It keeps on ticking
while I take the licking
and the next thing I find
I've lost track of time.

Hey Brother — before you go
can you lend me an ear?
Forget the time —
        can you tell me the year?

Blackout II

floating
in a sea
      of black
my memory is gone
will I get
      it back?
my mind is slipping
and it scares me so
when the only answer
I have is:
      "I don't know."

Oblivion

from existence
to extinction
in a flash

leaving only an instant
of recognition in its wake

where what was
meets
what no longer is

Dreamless

She listens to the ice-rain fall outside –

Feels the freezing wind blow
Through the window's pane

It is almost as cold as my heart,
She thinks.

And even though she is inside
She is neither safe nor warm

There is no shelter from my storm,
She thinks.

She falls asleep wondering
When her heart turned so cold

She does not dream.

III

At Times

I'm Moved to Beauty

Believing

I dream
I remember
I forget
I repress.
I scream
I surrender
I regret
I suppress.
I try
I run
I fight
I succeed.
I sigh
I won
I might
I believe.

Searching for the Light

Sitting in the darkness
searching for the light
to bring me to a place inside
where peace and safety are –

Where I can be myself
and like myself
for who I am
or
for who I am not.

Someday
that light will shine
and I will find
my way home.

Maybe

Maybe
in order to
find myself

I need to lose
myself.

Maybe
in order to
let go of the rage

I need to feel
the rage.

Maybe
in order to
gain control

I need to lose
control.

Maybe
in order to
believe in myself

I need to believe.

Learning to Live

It is difficult to
maintain the silence
that used to come easy.

My anger threatens
to explode at the
slightest provocation.

My whole body
is exhausted
by the effort needed
to hold onto myself.

It is time to let go —
time to stop dying
and learn to live.

Mid-Summer Musing

You put the blues in my country
Took the jazz from my soul
Gave me the classical feeling
Of having rock in my roll.
As I sit here in the bluegrass
And orchestrate my thoughts,
I write down the notes
Of the love songs I wrote
In honor of happiness sought.

The Cold Wind

The cold wind
sends a chill down my spine.

Though I know
the days will warm soon,
it seems so far away.

The blues and blahs of winter
have finally arrived,
calling for spring
to come ease the pains.

And yet
when the sun sets
through the clouds,
hanging huge and orange
in the sky —

And the whiteness
of the frozen land
reflects its own beauty,

Then the wind is not
quite as cold,
the chill does not run
quite as deep

and warm days
are only a vision away.

Hospital Visit

You go in thinking mom
will still be mom

but she's not.

Instead, you find a woman
who is agitated and confused,
struggling to make a
coherent sentence —
most of her thoughts
fading away half-spoken,
then silence.

Sometimes, her frustration
is evident.
Other times, she does not
seem to notice her lack of
completion.

She still looks like mom —
enough to know it's her

but her sharpness has dulled.

Hallucinations fill her head,
take shape in her mouth
and pass to my ears:

"There's a green head poking up now,"
she says with her eyes closed.
"And little green things above it."

She continues
describing the images
then opens her eyes,
turns her head to see me
and flashes a mischievous grin.

I smile back at her
and we both laugh.

For this moment, she is aware
of the absurdity bestowed
upon her.

For this moment
I love her
like I have never loved her before.

Subsequent Visits: The Kissing Lips

Please leave your lips
at the door
you won't need them
anymore.

At least not here
in this room
where germs abound
or may take bloom.

Please kindly leave
your lips right there –
we have for you
another pair

That you can use
when greeting mom
the kissing lips
will serve you strong.

You can kiss her
freely then
no need to worry
where you've been.

What you've been doing
or whom you've been with
will matter not
with the kissing lips.

But when you are done
and before you go, please
reclaim your own lips
on your way out the door.

Rummaging Around

Rummaging
                      around
          in the past
                            like an
old closet
                  or attic
          needing
                        to be
cleaned
                out.
Some things
                  to
                          throw
        some
            to
save —
            a lot
        to
                  pack
                        away —
neatly
            boxed up
          stacked
stored
                  for
                    a
            rainy
                day
          of
reminiscing.

What Truth Does She Hold

What truth does she hold
What lie does she keep
What stops her from saying
Is she buried that deep?

Whose hope keeps her going
Whose faith does she have
Who's threatening to beat her
Is she really that bad?

Why die to find freedom
Why live to feel pain
Why all these questions
When she's not to blame?

Some say forgive her
Some cry: It's a sin!
Yet some don't believe
When will it all end?

Tagged

Big
    Hot
        Wet
            Tears

Well-up and over
drop
      by
              drop
like children playing tag

"you're it!'

faster and faster until
the littlest one is tagged

"it's not fair!"

crying all the harder now.

Poem on the Run

A poem
ran through my head
the other day –

And wrote itself
before my very mind.

But it escapes me now.

Only pieces of it flash
before my eyes –
fragmented memories of
something that was,
for a moment,
all I could think about.

I tried to hold it in my head
until I could write it down.

But I waited too long.
It kept running
and my brain couldn't keep up.

No More Freud

I don't want to think like Freud anymore.

I want all my cigars
to be cigars –

not hidden words
with hidden meanings –

just thoughts
just feelings
straight up –
        not on the rocks.

No more slips
or complexes
stemming from the sexes

I just want what I say
to stay what I mean.

Nothing more.
Nothing less.

No further explanation
or exploration
needed.

Shoes

He's just a man.
Not a god or a demon.

I can tell by his shoes.

They are shoes any man would wear
bought at a five-and-dime
or through a mail order catalog.

I noticed them
when I was standing, talking to him one day –
feeling as I always feel when I'm around him:
      that he is not real
        that he is larger than life
            definitely larger than me.

Then I happened to glance down,
saw his shoes
and how ordinary they looked.
At that moment I realized –
He's just a man.

Not a god
Or a demon.

But a man –
who thought he was a god
and acted like a demon.

Crumbling

He is crumbling
under the weight
of his own creation.

He is aging
in the isolation
of his own making.

His body cannot
hold up to the
strains of living.

He is sagging from
the heaviness
of his own misgivings.

To Be Free is All I Ever Really Wanted

Only the mind knows
what is needed
to live a life
of survival.

Now, you say,
I don't have to
merely survive.

Now, you say,
I can live a new life
with answers
to questions
that have haunted me
since my time began.

And now I know
to be free
is all I ever really wanted.

The Lost and Found

F
 a
  l
   l
    e
     n

through the

    c
     r
    a
     c
    k
     s

landing flat on b r o k e n
backs

no way
               out
cause there's
no
way
up   alive but

u
n
d
e
r
ground

they are the lost   and never found.

Molten Rocket

Like the fiery sea at sunset
Like the mourning glory of day
Like the sand that sinks its teeth
into the drowning man's leg

Like the speeding bullet of death
Like the eye of the hurricane's storm
Like the gun that shoots nothing
but blank lines from the writer's pen

Misty morning tears
clearly show the way
out of one man's madness
and into the lull of his daughter's
goodbye

The rocket from beyond does not dance
like the ignited torch it touched
upon being lit

The drowning man's sorrows are
only bits and pieces of what remains
once the molten has cooled.

Blood, Snakes, and Mayonnaise

blood drips from the snake,
which is covered in mayonnaise

a dreadful combination
even in a dream

a mayo-blood-and-snake sandwich —
hold the cheese, please

but even the cheese has a head
and the tongue has a fork
and the bread goes uneaten —
the winners having soaked up
the sweat and tears of their rivals

it's just another sunday morning
in the garden

At Times I'm Moved to Beauty: A poem inspired by Emily Dickinson, Edna St. Vincent Millay, and Sylvia Plath

At Times I'm Moved to Beauty
By Tears of Recognition
When Sights and Sounds and Textures
Stir my Precognitions

Yearnings Peak, like Mountain Tops
Deep Aching Evokes my Soul
Foothills Serve as Stepping Stones
For Where I Want to Go

For Where I Want to Go is Up –
Away from Darkness' Grip
To Stand Upon the Rock of Strength
From Lightness, Take a Sip

And these Tears of Recognition
Now Move Me to No Bounds
Find Beauty in the Essence
Of My Textures, Sights, and Sounds.

Diamond in the Rough

There's always
a diamond
    in the rough
if you look
    hard enough.